A Season with Eagles

A Season with Eagles

Dr. Scott Nielsen

VOYAGEUR PRESS

Copyright © 1991 by Scott Nielsen

Printed in Hong Kong through Bookbuilders, Ltd.
First Hardcover Edition 91 92 93 94 95 5 4 3 2 1
First Softcover Edition 94 95 96 97 98 5 4 3 2 1

Library of Congress Cataloging-in-Publication Data
Nielsen, Scott,
    A season with eagles / Scott Nielsen.
        p.   cm.
    ISBN 0-89658-148-9
    ISBN 0-89658-247-7 (pbk.)
    1. Bald eagle.   2. Bald Eagle—Wisconsin.   I. Title
QL696.F32N54   1991
598.9'16—dc20   90-25444
                                                CIP

Voyageur Press books are also available at discounts for quantities for educational, fundraising, premium, or sales-promotion use.
For details contact the marketing department. Please write or call for our free catalog of natural history publications.

Published by
Voyageur Press, Inc.
P. O. Box 338
123 North Second Street
Stillwater, MN 55082 U.S.A.
In Minn 612-430-2210
Toll-free 800-888-9653

Distributed in Canada by
Raincoast Books
112 East Third Avenue
Vancouver, BC V5T 1C8

Book and cover design by Lou Gordon
Layout by Gordon Maltby
Edited by Helene Jones

Contents

Prologue

Many Americans first think of the bald eagle as the symbol of the United States, an embodiment of independence and power. Others think of the bird's menacing stare, fierce-looking beak, and aggressive disposition. Still others call to mind a vision of mythical strength such as the Thunderbird, the messenger between humankind and the afterlife, the slap of whose wings brought thunder to many of our North American Indian cultures. To a scientist, this species might be more recognizable by its scientific name, *Haliaeetus leucocephalus*, literally, "the sea eagle with a white head." And the tens of thousands of bald eagles in Canada should not be left out. The scientist knows that the eagle knows no political boundaries when it comes to finding a suitable home. Indeed, the experience presented in this book could just as well have been obtained in southern Ontario as in northern Wisconsin. The habitat and chronology of nesting is essentially identical in both places.

Symbol, myth, scientific specimen—I now think of the bald eagle as much more than these. For a season I was privileged to live with a pair of bald eagles near my Northwoods residence, watching as they courted, built a home, and raised a family with a tenderness and caring entirely at odds with my preconceived notions.

The season highlighted my wildlife-centered career. As an ornithologist, I was able to observe and describe many rarely seen aspects of the eagles' behavior. As a photographer, I was able to capture on film interactions of the eagles never before documented. But most important, as a fellow being traveling with them on the same planet, I was able to experience an elegance, simplicity, and vitality of living that in many ways pale our fretful human existence.

This book is a record of one season with the eagles. I wish you could have felt the first mild, late winter day when the birds' courting began in earnest; I wish you could have clung to the blind with me, shivering through the mid-April snowstorm that dumped eighteen inches of snow on the incubating female and her nest; I wish you could have shared my excitement as the first-hatched young eaglet opened its eyes and raised its head to survey the beautiful springtime world spread before it; and I wish you could have been with me when the same eaglet left its home and became a part of that new world one dog day morning in mid-July.

The Empire Wilderness area in northwestern Wisconsin.

This volume tries to capture some of that feeling, but I hope you use it not as a substitute for your own experience, but rather as an incentive to go out and see nature with your own eyes, feel it with your own hands, and know that you're a part of it all. Few of us will ever experience what I have with the eagles. The logistics and legalities of doing what I did in a way that would not disturb the birds were monumental; but regardless of where you live or how much time you have, an equally special part of nature waits for your personal discovery.

Until then, come share my season with the eagles.

In eagles, there is a marked size difference between the male and the female. Here, the larger female is on the left. Her head is more block-shaped in comparison to the male's smooth, rounded head.

The adult pair returned in late February at sunset and roosted on a dead birch tree near my home.

A Season with Eagles

We on the tundra of northern Wisconsin enjoy the area partly because of the four well-defined seasons: cold, snow, rain, and tough sledding. Calendars go out the window up here; nature tells us the seasons. Geese flying south means autumn, the first robin signals spring, nestling birds means summer, and the first flocks of redpolls and siskins means that winter's axe is about to fall. But of all the days I mark on my mental calendar, none is so important as the late February day my eagles return. They migrate south most winters. Although they can take any amount of cold, they haven't figured out how to fish through the ice, and until a few winter-killed deer become available later in the season, their winter home is the open waters of the St. Croix and Mississippi rivers, where food is plentiful.

During this particular year they showed up at sunset, taking their roost on a dead birch tree a few hundred yards away from where I was ice fishing. (Say what you will about your regal bald eagle, but they are not above taking an easy meal when they can get one, and it seemed they waited for handouts of cast-away fish.) They would, I hoped, have company this year. With federal and state permission, I had erected a blind at the broken-off top of a massive white pine tree the preceding fall, only 220 yards from where they had previously nested. I had hauled up a fifty-pound telephoto lens to the blind, which was some 105 feet high. There the thoroughly tested lens was lodged, giving me an eagle's eyesight and perspective. I had climbed and reclimbed that huge pine, memorizing every branch and foothold because, to avoid disturbing the birds, I could enter and leave the blind only in total darkness. But a million doubts went through my mind. Maybe the birds would choose a different one of their three nests this year; maybe one of several bad storms we had over the winter had toppled my observation tree; maybe something would happen to the eagles to keep them from nesting.

I left a few crappies on the ice as a goodwill offering for the eagles and headed home. My time for second-guessing had quickly come to an end, and my season with the eagles was about to begin.

✳ ✳ ✳

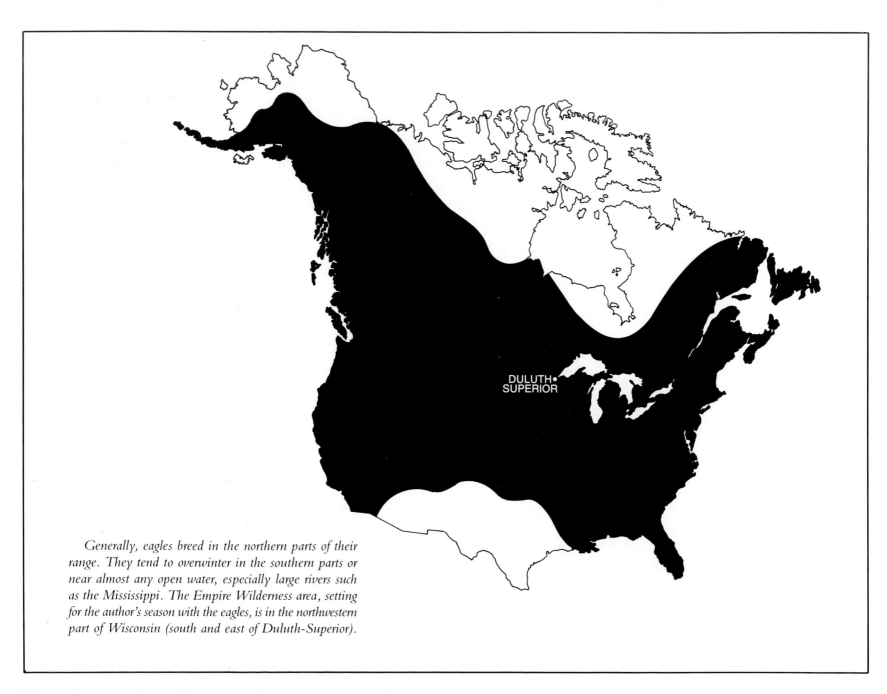

DULUTH •
SUPERIOR

Generally, eagles breed in the northern parts of their range. They tend to overwinter in the southern parts or near almost any open water, especially large rivers such as the Mississippi. The Empire Wilderness area, setting for the author's season with the eagles, is in the northwestern part of Wisconsin (south and east of Duluth-Superior).

"Be in your blind before dawn, don't leave until after dusk, and in between, make no sound other than breathing and the click of your camera shutter." The government's instructions to me seemed simple enough in the comfort of my home, but I was shaken into reality at 2:30 A.M. on an early March morning by the sound of my ringing alarm. No breakfast, because it would be impossible to go to the bathroom for the next sixteen hours. Just a half-dozen layers of clothing to combat the −20 degree Fahrenheit night, a forty-pound pack of camera bodies and film, a pair of snowshoes, and I was out the door, headed into the Empire Wilderness area.

The trip to the home I would share with the eagles for the next five months was less than two miles as the eagle flies, but it was a two-hour adventure through black spruce bog and cedar swamp for a land-based mammal like me. The Empire Wilderness is just about as wild an area as is found in the lower forty-eight states. Roads are infrequent. Bogs, swamps, and islands of pine rule here. Only the hoot of a barred owl and distant howling of the Empire pack of timber wolves broke the crunching sound of my snowshoes.

I thought often on my trips of the loggers who combed the same area at the turn of the century. Winter was their time to work in the woods, the frozen ground and layer of snow allowing them access to the otherwise isolated islands of pine. Fortunately for the eagles—and for myself—a few spots were difficult to reach even in winter, and some trees were spared. As I reached my pine tree, I imagined the timber cruiser who once would have stood where I was, gazing up at the gnarled and twisted pine, and finally deciding it just wasn't worth the effort to bring it down and haul it out. Easier pickings were much more numerous elsewhere. Its many branches, a disadvantage in logging, were ideal for my climbing. And its broken-off top allowed as stable a base as possible, considering I would be working with very sensitive equipment up more than ten stories in the air.

After a twenty-minute climb, I reached the top of my tree. Dawn was breaking, and the two hulklike forms of sleeping eagles perched alongside the distant nest confirmed that I had chosen the correct eyrie to photograph. You might think it difficult for an eagle to be inconspicuous, but by tucking its snow-white head under a wing while sleeping, it not only protects its head but also creates camouflage. And the two sleepers nearly seven hundred feet from me had chosen a roost tree in pro-

portion to their size. An eagle in a zoo can't help but stand out, yet perched in a massive pine tree, the three-foot length and seven-foot wingspan are almost lost amid branches that may be thirty-feet long and a foot in diameter.

The particular tree these eagles had chosen was a classic. A core I had taken from its base the winter before showed it to be 320 years old. With a circumference of fourteen feet at its base, it was a giant even in the logging days. But now it was showing its age. Blister rust had killed the topmost branches, which were bare and breaking off, and bark was beginning to slough from various places on the trunk. Pine trees grow much like people, with lots of growth in height during adolescence (which for a pine tree is the first one hundred years), followed by a filling out of girth in adulthood (another two hundred years for a pine), and then a weakening and shortening in old age, the period this pine was well into.

For the eagles, this tree was ideal for their nest. Eagles generally don't nest at the uppermost point of a tree because the branches there usually aren't strong enough to support a nest that could eventually grow to a ton or more. Like most eagles, these had chosen a strongly forked, large branch about twenty feet from the top. Into this crotch the first sticks were wedged. Often this is the most difficult stage of nest building. I've seen potential nest trees littered with branches at their bases and climbed them only to find unfinished nests, aborted simply because the first few sticks would not stay in place. Not so with this nest: Two side branches gave the eyrie a tripodlike stability, and over the years the nest had grown to a depth of five feet and a width of seven feet.

Even though it was not at the top of the tree, the nest was high enough up (ninety-five feet) to give the eagles a commanding view of the surrounding second-growth forest. The higher above ground eagles are, the more secure they feel, although in the far north they will use the ground for nesting when trees aren't available. My eagles had further opened the view by plucking most of the green pine sprigs from the support branches, removing obstructions as well as yielding a clear place to land.

The male, on the right, is conspicuous because of his white-feathered head. But eagles can camouflage themselves by tucking their heads under their wings. This photo was taken when egg laying was near. The female is in the "egg-laying lethargy state," while her mate stands guard next to her. She would be hard to spot were she alone.

Eagles prefer to locate their nest below the top of the tree, giving them a feeling of privacy.

The nest tree they chose was an old white pine spared by the loggers. In this picture, the male is at the top of the tree. The branch he is sitting on was killed by blister rust, a fungal infection that is fairly common throughout the white pine range. The female is perched alongside the nest.

Some nest-site turnover does occur. This was the second year that my two eagles used this nest, but if something happens to a pair of eagles so that neither returns for a nesting season, a new pair may well take over the nesting area, and they may use the same nest as the previous pair used. This isn't so much to save time and energy; eagles are compulsive nest builders and will likely add almost as much material to an already constructed nest as a new, from-scratch nest. Rather, within any particular nesting area, only a few locations are most ideal for a nest. These locations require a large tree with strong support branches, they must be isolated and near water, they must afford a clear view of the surroundings, and they must provide open flight paths to and from the tree. New pairs pick a location not so much because a nest is already there, but rather for the same reasons the previous pair selected the site.

A new pair in a home range doesn't occur often. If we assume a 10 percent annual mortality rate for adults each year, then one nest in ten will be home to a new adult each year. This will likely be a bird that has mated with the surviving eagle that used the nest in previous years. The chances of both adults dying in the same year are only one-tenth times one-tenth, or one in a hundred. That means in a state like Wisconsin, with about 250 nest territories, on average only two or three sites will be available to new pairs each year. Instead of using existing sites, new pairs are more likely to stake out new nest locations not occupied in recent years.

The pair at their nest, quiet and secluded. Note how large the nest is. It was constructed by using heavy, strongly forked branches near the top of the tree. The eagles almost always looked in opposite directions to guard against predators or disturbances, and snapped to attention whenever a sound was heard.

While I was observing the eagles, often I heard the same noise and witnessed the eagles' reaction. If a noise is bothersome to eagles, they often show it by leaving the nest site, an indication that they feel they are being intruded upon. However, I never saw my eagles react to sound by itself. Rather, the eagles' very acute hearing picked up every sound, and each sound was followed by close visual examination of wherever the sound came from. Only if visual scrutiny confirmed a threat would they leave the area. The eagles' use of visual confirmation of threats is interestingly evident in April when researchers commonly fly over nests to see which are being used. Often the pilots fly within a few hundred feet of the incubating birds, but the noisy planes don't bother the birds at all. The bird watches the plane but does not visually recognize it as a threat. An egg-eating gull quietly soaring overhead elicits much more of a reaction from the eagle than the noisy plane does.

It's almost impossible to sneak up on a lone eagle, and forget about doing it with two on the watch. The birds had roused themselves from that night's sleep, and I observed how they immediately faced in opposite directions, giving them a combined 360-degree field of view. They kept these sentry positions for most of the day. Any noise immediately got the eagles' attention. Their acute hearing picked up every sound: a red squirrel crunching along the snow, a nuthatch poking around the nearby bark. Each sound was followed up by a close visual examination of the area from which it came, and if visual observation confirmed any threat, both birds would steal off into the distance.

In the five weeks from late February until the end of March, the eagles repaired their nest, did their courting and mating, and prepared for egg laying. These daily tasks took only a few hours; most of the rest of the time was spent perched at the eyrie, scanning the area. Once eggs are in the nest, eagles have a fifteen-week commitment until the young leave, and I got the feeling that March's nest-area surveying was very much to minimize the chances that interferences would arise from April through July. The loss of a single nearby tree or the passage of a human or other disturbance through the area might have been enough to cause them to abandon the nest at this early stage. From seeing how they scrutinized everyday things so thoroughly, it became clear to me why I had to be so thorough in my preparations and actions in order not to interfere with them.

Bald eagles are compulsive nest builders: Their eyries are some of the largest of all birds'. Both male and female do the initial nest building, and the pair works together to refurbish an old nest if they intend to reuse it that season. Sticks and dead branches from nearby trees are the most common nest materials. I often saw one of the birds leave the tree, heard a loud snap, and a few moments later watched the bird return with a branch in its claws. With a weight of ten pounds and a loafing flight speed of thirty miles per hour, an eagle packs quite a punch and uses this momentum to snap off branches from the tops of the nearby trees. I've seen branches up to six or seven feet in length brought to the nest and then taken in the bird's beak and added to the ever-growing platform.

Grasses, cattails, mosses, and other plant matter are also worked into the nest to fill in any gaps between the branches. Working for an hour or two each morning

The pair works together early in the season to arrange nest materials. The eagles start in early March; note the snow on the nest. Only the horned owl and, occasionally, the goshawk nest earlier. Eagles move into their nests early because of the long nesting season. Twenty weeks will pass from the time they return until the young fledge, and the young won't be on their own until ten weeks after fledging.

Sunrise around the eagles' nest tree. The tree, chosen for its isolation from likely disturbances and proximity to water, appears as a silhouette above the height of the surrounding second-growth forest.

and again in the afternoon, a pair of bald eagles can construct a complete nest in less than a week or refurbish an old nest in a day or two. Refurbishing involves building an approximately foot-high rim of sticks and grasses around the nest edge, forming a bowl in the center to hold the eggs. It's hard to imagine how a seemingly slapdash group of sticks and grasses could hold together, but the settling that occurs locks everything in place as solidly as the best beaver dam.

When watching their nest refurbishing, it didn't take me long to tell the male from the female. As with most birds of prey, the female is about a third heavier than her mate (a condition ornithologists refer to as reverse sexual dimorphism because among birds males are generally larger than females). This made it easy to tell the birds apart when they were side by side. Individually, the female has a bulkier, squarer build. I especially noticed the difference in their heads: The smooth, rounded one of the male contrasted with the rough, squarish female's.

Eagles, compulsive nest builders, use sticks, short ones and long ones, to build a nest whose rim will be eight to twelve feet high. Grasses are also used for nest building and refurbishing. As twigs and grasses are added to the nest, the birds work their bodies down into the center to help form a bowl into which the eggs will be laid. The birds close their wings, close their talons, and lower themselves into the bowl with a side-to-side motion to smooth out any irregularities. The bowl is thus shaped not only to hold eggs but also to fit the bodies of the adults. Here the female is screaming at the male because she's coming into breeding condition.

The birds use their bills to carry sticks around the nest and to position them. The female is paying more and more attention to the male (obvious in this picture), which is a sign of her coming into breeding condition.

Much has been written about why, in many raptor species, the female is larger than the male. One old theory holds that this allows the female to successfully protect her young from a possibly aggressive male, but this simply doesn't apply to the bald eagle. The answer to size differences probably lies in flight dynamics. Although eagles do feed on carrion, freshly killed food makes up a good part of their diet, especially during the nesting season. The male's smaller size enables him to maneuver, and therefore he is more adept at catching live prey and does most of the hunting for the young eaglets while the female almost constantly attends the nest to protect the young during their first few weeks of life.

Nest refurbishing was essentially complete by mid-March, and now only the male brought nest-making materials. It's believed that captive male eagles continue to bring materials to the nest in order to bring the female into breeding condition, and my experiences in the wild confirmed the idea. As the first day of spring approached, the female became more and more vocal anytime the male arrived with materials. To these vocalizations she later added a fluffing of her feathers and shaking of her body. It didn't matter how large or small the amount of materials: His bringing a footful of grasses elicited as much of a response as a large branch did.

This continued for a week until, on March 20, the first mating took place. The event was one of fruition, almost relief, for me; it was confirmation that the steps I had taken to avoid disturbing the birds had been sufficient to allow their natural behavior to occur. It began with the female perched on one of the nest-support branches and the male settled down into the nest cup, and I could see only his head and part of his back. As the female came into a receptive condition, she screamed at the male, inciting him to leave the nest for sticks and grasses. He returned a minute later with a large birch stick, which elicited the vocalizing, fluffing, and shaking I had now become familiar with. As the male arranged the branch, the female hopped to one of her favorite roosts and pronated herself on the large branch. This soliciting posture soon brought the male to her side, and after checking the area for any disturbance, he hopped on her back, and mating began.

The eagles keep near-continual sentry duty, looking for any possible disturbance throughout the nesting season. Humans are perhaps the greatest irritant to prenesting adults. In virtually all cases, any sight of humans will cause the eagles to leave the nest area, which can result in abandonment of the nest for that season. This early in the season, self-preservation takes precedence over nesting success. However, such disturbances after the young are two to three weeks old are less likely to result in nest desertion, provided the disturbance is brief.

He wrapped his talons around the female's wings where they joined her body (this spot is near the bird's center of gravity when she is in a pronated position, and the positioning of the male here allows the female to stay in balance), flapping his wings to maintain balance. Slowly the female again lowered herself into the pronated position so that the male could work his tail under the female's and deposit sperm. Then it was the male's turn to be vocal during mating, which lasted ten to twenty seconds, after which he hopped off and perched near the female. After giving a "high call" or two, in which her head was held high above her back, and intently watching the now-alert male as he stretched his wings, the female became quite lethargic. This "postcopulation lethargy" on the part of the female is possibly important in allowing the male's sperm to migrate up her cloacal opening into the oviduct because the male lacks a penis and cannot deposit the sperm deeply. Any big movements on the part of the female right after mating could accidentally dislodge the sperm.

The male's talons could have been a danger to the female during the mating. More than once I observed several of her wing covert feathers attached to his talons after mating; especially when mounting, the female would pull a translucent nictitating membrane, a sort of a third eyelid, up over her eyes to protect them.

The eagles mated two or three times each morning and afternoon. I observed close to forty matings, all starting with the male bringing materials to the nest and all occurring with the female perched on one of the nest support branches. From my lofty blind I gained an appreciation for the importance of the male's bringing nest materials prior to mating. In one particular case, the male brought a branch, and the female assumed a soliciting posture, which she held for upwards of a minute while the male arranged his branch in the nest. When he failed to join her, she circled the nest back to another perch and no mating occurred until an hour later when he returned with another branch. I witnessed a very ritualized, elegant interaction between the birds, but one which the slightest disturbance or mistiming could interrupt.

These next ten photographs show the pair keeping the same ritual that eagles have followed for millions of years. A second sequence follows this first.

Eagle copulation sequence 1: *When the male brings nest material, the female becomes quite excited and hops to an adjacent support branch.*

Eagle copulation sequence 1: *At the adjacent support branch, she assumes a pronated soliciting posture while the male arranges the stick he brought in the nest.*

Eagle copulation sequence 1: *The critical timing not lost, the male hops to her side and then on her back, grabbing the female's wings near where they join her body. When the female is in the pronated position, this spot is near her center of gravity.*

Eagle copulation sequence 1: *Copulation is occurring. He flaps his wings to balance himself.*

Eagle copulation sequence 1: *The male hops off the female.*

Eagle copulation sequence 1: *After copulation, the female gives a screamlike "high call," holding her head over her back, which she commonly did after copulation.*

Eagle copulation sequence 1: *The female continues to pay attention to the male, watching him stretch his wings.*

Eagle copulation sequence 1: *Again, she shows her interest in the male, watching him scratch.*

Eagle copulation sequence 1: *The female is screaming at the male, common after copulation.*

Eagle copulation sequence 1: *After copulation, the female crouches into a postcopulation lethargy posture, perhaps to allow sperm to migrate up the cloacal opening into the oviduct. The male is preparing to take flight, while the lethargic female remains near the nest.*

Eagles must live near open water, and much of the Wisconsin eagle population will head south along the Mississippi River for the winter.

An old folk tale says that eagles mate in the air, but the weight of the birds and the necessity for accurate cloacal touching makes this impossible, although it is a romantic thought. A certain amount of courtship is probably done during the few hours at midday when the eagles leave the nest to do their feeding. The eagles may court with undulating, roller coaster flight, catching thermals and rising out of sight, then tumbling downward to earth. But during my season with the eagles, it was clear that much of the courting and mating activity occurred at or near the nest because this was where the birds spent most of their time and felt most secure.

Occasionally a pair of eagles dies after hitting a power line or the ground, their talons locked together. When this occurs to a pair it is likely a courtship maneuver, although the same locking of talons may occur when one of the mated pair attempts to chase an intruder out of the nest territory. Talons, which are attached to powerful leg muscles, are an eagle's main means of catching prey and defending itself. When an intruder is spotted, an adult will commonly make a direct flight to the intruder and stoop or dive at the intruder to chase it away. It might also approach the trespasser from below or at the same level, and in these cases the adult often flips sideways or even upside down and extends its feet and talons at the intruder. In doing this, the birds occasionally become entangled, whether intentionally or accidentally, and drop some distance through the air before freeing themselves, if they have time.

As March drew to a close, the female's postcopulation lethargy, which at first had showed for up to a half hour after mating, evolved into a near-sickness that lasted for several hours at a time. It was clear that eggs were forming inside her, and she would spend most of the daylight hours in the same sleeping posture, a tucked-under head, that I had become so familiar with during the night. Perhaps this "egg-laying lethargy" period is the most delicate stage of the nest cycle. The female stayed at the nest twenty-four hours a day, and the male brought her food once or twice a day. This one-week period of egg-laying lethargy and egg laying itself was the only time I saw either adult bird bring food to the nest for the other adult, although, of course, the adults do bring food for the eaglets. Up until this point, both birds were gone at midday, probably to a carcass of a winter-killed deer that they could feed on.

Eagle copulation sequence 2: *This second copulation occurred on a different support branch. The male has deposited the nest material and has flown to the female's side. Together, the pair will check to make sure there are no disturbances nearby.*

Eagle copulation sequence 2: *The birds bow to each other. The female already has the nictitating membrane drawn over her left eye to prevent damage when the male mounts her. Pulling the nictitating membranes over the eyes can be a reflex, much as humans blink their eyes when something comes close to them, or it can be intentional as it is in this case.*

Eagle copulation sequence 2: *Copulation is occurring.*

Eagle copulation sequence 2: *The female is again giving the postcopulatory "high call."*

The pair has returned to their nest tree in the early afternoon after spending the midday hunting The female has already perched and the male, his bulging crop evident, is landing. She is screaming at the male, her head turned so that she can see him.

The size of the eagles' home range is mainly determined by assurance of an adequate food supply. Within this large home range, eagles will set up their territory based on where they find the most suitable nest trees. The territory can be anywhere within the home range; it doesn't have to be centered in the home range. The location of the home range is largely determined by where the food is. For the bald eagle, which feeds primarily on fish during the nesting season, the home range must encompass lakes and rivers. The location of these lakes and rivers in the area will determine where the eagles feed and hence their flight paths to and from the nest.

Deer are a staple in the diet of Northwoods eagles when the eagles return in the spring, before the ice has left the lakes. A pound of food is all that is needed for an adult eagle each day; a few winter-killed deer and other prey give them a full diet for several months, so finding enough to eat is not a problem. I often observed them in the early afternoon returning from a day's feeding with bulging crops and bloodied head feathers. Indeed, one danger to eagles at this time of year is the road-killed deer left to lie along the highways. A gorged eagle feeding on such an animal is slow to take flight, encumbered by the extra one or two pounds of its meal, and every season eagles are hit by cars as they attempt to lumber into flight from a road-side carcass.

Eagles typically lay two eggs, spaced around four days apart, and in the Northwoods the first egg is in the nest by April 1. The female starts incubation immediately after the laying of the first egg, so that it is four days along in its development by the time the second one is laid. My eagles followed this same pattern. The female did all the incubating until the second egg was laid, with the male generally perched in a nearby "loafing" tree, coming to the nest only to bring food for the female.

I was amazed at how inactive the nest appeared to be during this time. The deep well of the nest cup swallowed up the female as well as her first-laid egg; even though I was ten feet above the nest level I could rarely see more than a few white head feathers. At any noise she would lift her head just enough to let her yellow eyes inspect for danger, and every few hours she would raise herself enough to turn the egg and reposition herself to ensure even incubation.

It was at this time that I realized another advantage of nesting below the very top of the tree. Egg-eating gulls and crows were now returning to the area, and the overhanging branches above the nest provided excellent camouflage for the nest and the eggs it contained. The female occasionally squawked at the intruders, and any real threat could be dealt with if necessary by chasing the animal, usually, and sometimes by attacking. (Humans are a different story: In virtually all cases, any sign of people will cause the eagles to leave the nest area instead of attacking.) But by and large eagles prefer to avoid a fight, and the camouflage the large pine afforded my eagles helped to prevent conflicts.

Both birds have spied a red squirrel running along the snow ninety-five feet below them. All movements like this, no matter how harmless, are noted and examined by the pair. Because pine and other conifer cones are a staple in its diet, the red squirrel is a common species in eagle country, and it often poses a threat to the eagles' eggs.

A ring of white excrement, such as is leaving the female in this picture, quickly forms around the base of an active nest tree. Indeed, such telltale whitewashing around the tree is a good clue to ground-based researchers that the nest is currently being used.

Gray squirrels are threats as well. I caught a gray squirrel scurrying around in the nest and on the adjacent branch, probing for eggs or other food. The eagles were lucky this time. This photograph was taken in March when the adults were gone at midday, before eggs were in the nest. Later, they'll have to be more careful. It is mandatory that at least one adult be at the nest at all times during incubation to guard against egg-eating predators like gray squirrels.

Here, the pair is vocalizing to each other after copulation. Eagles continue to copulate very close to the time of egg laying. To avoid any possible disturbance of the already pregnancy-sick female, I did not photograph her during actual egg laying.

Unpaired and immature bald eagles also passed through the Northwoods during incubation, but they were quickly driven off by the male. The territory eagles defend is not huge; it is generally an area of only a square mile within eyesight of the nest. In even the densest bald eagle concentrations in Alaska, nests of separate pairs are not found within less than a mile or two of each other. But for bald eagles a more useful concept than territory is the idea of a home range, the ten- to fifteen-square-mile area that they cover in obtaining their food and in which the young spend a month or two after fledging. If prey is abundant, or large numbers of eagles are present, the home range may approach the size of the territory. The two to three nests an eagle pair uses can be anywhere within this home range. This territory-within-a-home-range is a very flexible arrangement, allowing the birds both a choice of nesting locations as well as a diverse food supply.

Once the second egg was laid, the female came out of her lethargy and took turns with the male in incubating the eggs. He generally incubated for only a few hours at midday while the female went off to bathe, preen, and feed herself. The changing of the guard was different at each time of day. In the late morning, the female practically hopped off the eggs as soon as the male landed to take his turn. She had been on the eggs for perhaps twenty hours straight and was clearly anxious to have some free time. Conversely, when she returned at midafternoon, the male was often quite reluctant to leave the eggs. More than once I observed the female push her mate off them.

The necessity for constant incubation and presence of at least one bird at the nest was clear to me from an earlier experience in March. The pair had left for their midday hunt, and a gray squirrel found its way into the nest. He spent a half hour probing and sifting through every nook and cranny of the nest, looking for eggs, and I have no doubt that, had unguarded eggs been present then, he would have found and consumed them.

✳ ✳ ✳

In the next ten photographs, the eagles are incubating their two eggs. The first egg was laid in the first part of April; the second egg followed four days later.

Incubation: Early in April during a small snowstorm. The eggs need to be protected from below-freezing temperatures. Wood is a fairly good insulator, which helps trap the incubating parent's heat and keep it in the nest bowl.

Incubation: *Taken the morning after the big mid-April snowstorm that dumped eighteen inches of snow on the area—including the eagles, the eggs, and me.*

I had been fortunate so far in picking suitable days to be in my blind. Any outdoor photographer needs to be as much meteorologist as naturalist. My main concern was wind because any breeze over ten miles per hour caused my lens to sway too much to take sharp photographs.

My luck ran out in mid-April when a freak snowstorm moved in at midday and, in the next thirty hours, dumped eighteen inches of snow on the surrounding forest, the eagles' nest, and me. It is suicide to try to climb up and down a pine tree with snow-laden or wet branches. Foot pressure turns snow to the slickest ice imaginable, and my chances of making it down the tree in one piece were nil. I had no choice but to ride out the storm and its thirty-mile-per-hour winds.

It was quite a roller coaster ride. I had a rope to tie myself into the blind, and I did get a few hours sleep. Snow and wind raged all the next day, making photography impossible, but giving me one more day to admire how easily the eagles took it in stride. They didn't bother feeding that day, but they didn't need to: A healthy eagle can easily go for a week without food. They exchanged incubation duties as usual and seemed to enjoy the terrible weather that prevented any sane person from being in the area—except for a balding ornithologist roped to a tree an eighth of a mile away. They let down their guard a bit that day, and with no photography for me to concern myself with, I opened up my mind a bit too. It was a great day to be alive and perched in the treetops with the eagles. In Duluth, Minnesota, some thirty miles north of my spot, schools were closed, traffic was snarled, and tempers no doubt were flaring. For me and the eagles, it was probably as close to heaven as we'll get on this earth.

The snow let up in late afternoon and brought me back to reality. Wisconsin weather is truly unpredictable, but one sure thing is that high pressure comes in after any big snowstorm, clears the night sky, and temperatures drop out of sight. A fresh layer of pure white snow reflects any daytime heat, and the fairly balmy 25 degree afternoon became a −15 degree mid-April chiller just after sundown. It was still impossible to leave my blind, so after a meal of fresh snow, the eagles and I spent another night together.

Incubation: *A sound was heard. If the female feels threatened, she may start to scream, and such screaming usually brings the male to the rescue from nearby. Perhaps he will then have to drive off circling gulls while the female covers and shields the eggs.*

Incubation: *The adult normally sits low in the nest during incubation. If it hears a sound, it will raise its head to investigate.*

Incubation: *This was taken near the end of the incubation period, in late April. The sun was getting higher in the sky by this time, and the female is panting from the heat. Branches above the nest helped to shield her, except for a few hours in the day when the sun shone down through an open spot.*

The third day dawned cold, bright, dead quiet, and sky blue—perfect for photography. What a wondrous sight as the early light of dawn made the snow-covered nest glow. As the first rays of sunlight reached the nest, the female poked her white head up out of the snow to greet the morning. I was breathless. I'd traveled the globe and seen everything I ever thought I'd see. But the snow, the cold, the stillness, the quiet, the sun, the eagle's white head, the new life beneath her: That one scene summed up to me the specialness of life and I hoped my frostbitten fingers would work well enough to capture it on film.

The day quickly warmed to above freezing, and the sun melted the snow on the branches enough to dry them for my descent. My longest stand with the eagles was over, and permanent loss of part of a finger to frostbite would keep me sidelined for the next week, but I resolved to make it back in time for hatching.

Incubation: *The male relieves the female from incubation for a few hours at midday so that she can feed herself. The female has returned to the nest, but the male is reluctant to leave the eggs. She is screaming at him, perhaps to encourage him to leave the nest.*

Incubation: *She is preparing to push the reluctant male off the eggs. No one knows exactly how long it takes for an eagle egg to develop inside its mother. For the domestic chicken, it takes only a day for the egg to be released from the ovary, fertilized, have its yolk and shell formed, and then be laid. For the larger egg of an eagle, this time is no doubt longer. Mating begins in earnest about ten days before the first egg is laid, giving us a time limit of one to ten days for gestation.*

Incubation: *She has again returned to the nest. Blood from a recent meal clearly shows on her beak and some feathers. Eagles do wash themselves. They wade into shallow water and cover any soiled feathers with water, then fly to a nearby perch to dry and preen the feathers. Eagles are quite secretive in their bathing; it's one of the few times they are exposed to ground predators, so it isn't an activity seen often.*

Incubation: *Hatching is near. The male spends more time at the nest now and the female sits higher up, an indication that she is feeling movement in the eggs.*

Incubation: *Males occasionally add a few green sprigs of pine to the nest at the time of hatching. Here, the male has brought cattails to the nest. Some nest materials are brought throughout incubation, and the male's activity picks up when hatching nears.*

May 5 was the date. Five weeks after the first egg was laid, it hatched. At dawn I immediately knew that something was afoot. The male was perched at the nest instead of in a nearby roost tree as he had during incubation, and the female didn't sit as low down in the nest cup as before; she was in a brooding posture, just off the eggs, rather than an incubating one.

Although the just-hatched eaglet was much too small to be seen above the nest cup, I could follow the movements of both adults' heads as they, in unison, watched the squirming infant as it left its elliptical, tennis ball–sized shell. Occasionally, the male brought a sprig of green pine needles to the nest. He started this during incubation, and now several sprigs were added each day. Only the eagle knows exactly why it adds the pine boughs. Biologists used to think that these boughs served to deodorize the nest, but eagle nests are usually quite clean until the young start feeding themselves. Some people think that the sprigs decorate the nest, and although they do, we will never know how the eagles feel about them. I've noticed that the sprigs do help to camouflage the nest, breaking up the large, fairly uniform brown layer of sticks, and this could be important when eggs and young are in the nest. Also, the pine boughs might be useful in shading the young eaglet. My eaglet's light gray covering of natal down, although highly reflective, was still poor protection against the direct rays of the sun. Its parents always brooded in such a manner that the eaglet was shaded, and they moved the nearby pine sprigs around from time to time, possibly for the same purpose. Some biologists have suggested that as the fresh greenery decays, it generates enough heat to help keep the eggs and young warm from below. Yet another theory holds that the sprigs inhibit bacterial growth and thus are a small help in nest sanitation. While the adults are fairly scrupulous in picking up any scraps of food that the young refuses, for the first week the excrement of the eaglet is deposited in the nest bowl as opposed to being ejected out of the nest, and a layer of greenery could help in sanitizing this waste.

Hatching of the first-laid egg is occurring. The parents' interest is evident from their staring down into the nest bowl.

Natal down is also poor insulation against cool nighttime temperatures. During its first week of life the eaglet was brooded almost continuously; every hour or two the female raised herself up to feed a few small, saliva-rich morsels to the eaglet, only to resume brooding. Saliva is the means for passive antibody transfer from adult to newborn, much the same as mammalian mothers' milk is the vehicle for transfer of colostrum, which bolsters the immune system of the newborns during the first few hours of life.

By this time a bond had started to form between the adults and their offspring. During these early days, known as the "eyas" stage of development, feedings were the occasions and incentives for the adults bonding to the eaglet. Chances of nest desertion are high until the eaglet is past two weeks of age. After this point, most eagle pairs will tolerate a limited amount of disturbance, such as banding, without abandoning the nest. And by this first week the eaglet's eyes were open. Through a process known as imprinting, the eaglet was learning to recognize members of its own species by fixating on the sights and sounds of its parents.

Its nestmate had hatched around May 9, and was therefore about four days behind in development. When the firstborn eaglet was in its second week, dark gray juvenile down became noticeable as it came in amidst the lighter natal down. This darker down has better insulation properties, but is still poor protection against the sun, and shading and brooding were still necessary. The overhanging branches of the pine tree also helped with the shading, especially when the sun was highest at midday. This is another reason for the nest to be placed below the top of the tree, under protective branches.

On hot days the female brought grasses soaked in water. She did this all through incubation when she returned to the nest in the early afternoon, probably to control both the humidity and temperature in the nest bowl. Bald eagle eggs, like most other birds' eggs, have a narrow range of humidity and temperature tolerances for successful embryo development. For bald eagles, a temperature around 91 degrees Fahrenheit and relative humidity of 50 to 70 percent allow an air cell to form at the pointed end of the egg, through which the embryo can breathe before it actually hatches. Air weighs less than the initial egg material, and formation of this pocket results in bald eagle eggs losing about 15 percent of their initial, post-laying weight during incubation, which is about four or five ounces.

Now that the first egg has hatched, the female sits quite high in the nest in a brooding, rather than incubating, posture so as not to crush or smother the nestling.

Eagle country.

The male is bringing a stick to the nest during hatching of the second egg. The female closely covers the not-quite-yet-hatched egg and the eaglet to prevent the male from damaging them during landing. Three to four days pass between the hatching of the first and second eggs; thus, brooding and incubation occur at the same time.

Parents at the nest during hatching of the second egg.

The female is screaming again at passing gulls while protecting the newborn eaglet. Gulls are very aggressive, opportunistic birds and are definite threats to unprotected eggs and probably also to very young eaglets.

Imprinting and bonding: *Feedings are the occasions that foster imprinting and bonding. Imprinting occurs within the brain of the eaglet. When its eyes open after hatching, an eaglet fixates on the first moving thing it sees, which is its parent. Imprinting quickly follows, progressing in a brief period a few days after hatching. During this period, the range of objects to which the eaglet will respond significantly narrows. The eaglet does not learn to recognize its parents specifically; rather, it learns to recognize another of its species and learns to recognize itself as an eagle. Once imprinted, the eaglet will accept food from any eagle but tend to retreat from any other moving object.*

Bonding, on the other hand, occurs within the brain of the parent. Through feeding the young, the parents form a stronger attachment to the eaglet and the nest. Before eggs are in the nest, nothing ties the adults to the nest, and chances of desertion of the area are good if disturbance occurs. If disturbed repeatedly before young are in the nest, the adults may relocate to another of their nests or abandon their home range entirely. Only when a moving eaglet is in the nest, begging for food and being fed, can complete bonding occur.

In this photo, the female has torn off a piece of food and is feeding it to her eaglet.

The two-week-old eaglet was finally strong enough to hold its head up for feeding and to look around the nest area. Feedings occurred every three to four hours, and I could hear healthy begging calls from the eaglet prior to feeding. Up to now it would defecate in the nest, but at two weeks of age, the eaglet would instinctively back up to the edge of the nest and squirt its excrement over the side, much like its parents.

✳ ✳ ✳

Up until now, I had seen the eaglets only from a distance. But because I was able to obtain federal and state permission to accompany a licensed eagle bander to the eyrie, soon I would be in the nest with the same birds I saw created barely two months before.

Memorial Day weekend is the traditional start of eagle-banding activities in the Northwoods. Although, from this age on, most adult pairs will tolerate some disturbance, we still needed to take some caution. The trip in could last no more than a half hour, it could not be in cold weather when the eaglets might get chilled, and feedings could not be interrupted. I was allowed up the tree first while the bander prepared his gear and checked the ground beneath the nest for food remains to analyze the eagles' diet. I don't know who was more surprised when my head poked up above the nest rim, the funny-looking eaglets I saw or me, the first person they ever laid eyes on. My first impression was how big the three-week-old eaglets were. They were a full foot in height and about five pounds in weight, and I could see why this was referred to as the "ugly duckling" stage of their development. The almost fully grown feet, eyes, and beak left no doubt as to the regal birds these eaglets would become. But a stubby, fat body and short wings made everything out of proportion and it seemed impossible to me that such ungainly birds would be taking wing in only seven more weeks.

I was able to get a close-up look at my two birds. The first brown juvenile feathers were starting to appear, especially on the backs of the birds where the feathers protected against the sun and insulated against the cold, better than the natal down the feathers were pushing out. Gray juvenile down still covered most of the rest

Imprinting and bonding: *Although bonding and imprinting occur at about the same time, they are two very different things. Biologists use this knowledge in several areas of bald eagle management. Once imprinting has occurred and the eaglet recognizes itself as an eagle, wildlife managers can remove the eaglets from areas of healthy eagle populations, such as Wisconsin, and transfer them to nests in areas of low population. The eaglet accepts its new parents and the adults accept and bond to the fostered eaglet. Adults do not recognize their own young; they have no known sense of smell such as what cattle use to identify their own calves.*

Biologists will let eagle pairs that are known to lay infertile eggs incubate for five weeks or so, and then they will visit the nest to quickly switch the infertile eggs with young eaglets that were perhaps hatched in captivity. The parents come back, assume the eggs have hatched, and feed the young as if they were their own. And sometimes an eaglet is fostered into nests with other eaglets. Biologists try to keep the ages fairly close to avoid a much older bird outcompeting a much younger bird for food. If young are taken from a nest to be fostered into another nest, never are all the young taken from the donor nest. At least one young bird is left for the parents to raise. It's believed that allowing the eagles to complete a nesting and rearing cycle encourages them to return to the same area the next year and successfully raise a new brood.

In this photo, the eaglet takes a first view out of the nest under watchful eye of the mother.

Eagle banding: *A classic photo of three-week-old eaglets at the "ugly duckling" stage.*

The eaglets receive standard bands from the government. Every band has a unique number: The information about the band—location of eyrie, sex (if known), the band's number, etc.—is put into a computer in Laurel, Maryland, and retrieved when and if a band is recovered, generally when a bird is found dead. Occasionally, injured or sick birds are found with bands, the information obtained is sent to Maryland, and the banded bird, returned to health, is released. Most states hire banders for their eagle-banding programs, and about 90 percent of all the eaglets hatched in the continental United States are banded. Several banding programs are ongoing in Canada and Alaska, but the large numbers of nesting eagles and the wild country in those areas result in a smaller percentage of the population being banded.

Eagle banding: *A two-and-one-half-week-old eaglet with juvenile down well grown in. This is the earliest stage at which nests are visited by licensed ornithologists to band the birds. Biologists use their knowledge of imprinting and bonding to time their visits to the nest to keep the chances of nest desertion to an absolute minimum. They wait until the eaglets are two to three weeks of age—after bonding has occurred.*

of the body, and tufts of natal down occurred in spots here and there, especially on the top of the head. The eagles were hodgepodges of proportions and feathers, something put together by a committee.

If an eagle bander approaches a nest that contains young less than five weeks old such as ours held, the parent in attendance will typically flush, circle above the nest tree for a few minutes, and perch in a tree a safe distance away but within eyesight of the nest tree. And after the eaglets are five weeks old, both parents may be absent from the area and may not even be aware of the bander's visit. Our birds put up little fuss during the banding. The older bird could sit up and move its feet in a striking posture, but with undeveloped muscles to back them up, his bark was worse than his bite. A check of the nest showed a few sprigs of aspen leaves amid the normal nest materials, and pellets of deer fur confirmed the prey's importance in the birds' diet so far.

In the next week I visited several other Douglas County nests with the banders. Each of the sites was different, but all were equally beautiful and peaceful. Bald eagle young rarely fight among each other as, for instance, golden eaglets do. The "Cain and Abel" battles that occur among some raptor young and lead to the death of the younger sibling are rare among bald eagles. As long as each eaglet is fed sufficiently and nothing happens to the adults, the number of birds that survives through hatching is generally the same number that leaves the nest ten weeks later. In broods of three and, rarely, four eaglets, an occasional death of the youngest eaglet (the runt of the brood) is due not to intentional physical injury from its larger siblings but rather from its nestmates monopolizing the attention of the parents during feeding. Adults do not make an attempt to feed each eaglet equally, but rather they respond to whoever begs the most aggressively—commonly the firstborn, and hence oldest and largest, eaglets. In its first few days of life, a third or fourth eaglet may thus succumb to starvation when its older nestmates are three to five times larger and able to be more aggressive during feeding. This size difference is quickly made up by the time the youngest eaglet is two to three weeks old, when it is more able to compete equally for the parents' attention.

Eagle banding: Feeding the three-week-old eaglet.
Banding is not injurious to the eaglets. By the time the banders get to the birds, the eaglets' legs and feet are approaching adult size and a band can be placed that won't fall off yet will be large enough to not constrict the fully grown foot. Banding gives biologists an accurate means of censusing the population; it tells them about migratory patterns and gives them a good idea of typical eagle lifetimes. Often, at the same time that eagles are banded, one or two assistants comb the ground looking for prey remains, a good clue to the diet of the birds. The condition of the nest is checked because, as trees age, the limbs may need reinforcing to hold the ever-growing nest. Tree inspection during banding can lead to maintenance during the following winter. Blood samples are sometimes taken from the eaglets to check for lead, mercury, and other harmful poisoning.

Eagle banding: An adult circles over the nest tree during a banding visit.

The most unusual situation we encountered when banding came when we scaled up to an eyrie in which the older eaglet had been fed a piece of fish with a hook and monofilament line still attached. Eagles commonly pick up such fish because the fish die or are weakened and float on the water surface, making an easy target for eagles. In most cases, however, the adult will dissect out the hook and line before feeding it to the young. It became routine for us to find strands of fishing line dangling from the nest tree and a few fishing lures on the ground beneath the nest tree or nearby roost trees.

In this eaglet, however, the hook had become embedded in its crop with the remaining ten feet of line tightly wrapped around the bird's body, left wing, and left leg. It was a goner unless something was done. Unexpectedly, I was given the opportunity to use my training from an earlier career—dentistry. Although the last thing I expected to find myself doing was oral surgery ninety feet up a pine in the middle of nowhere, out came the hemostat from my camera kit, and the hook was removed, the line untangled. It was fortunately a barbless hook, and no bleeding occurred on removal, and we decided to leave the eaglet in the nest instead of transferring it to veterinary care. I checked that nest from a distance every few weeks, and the bird did fledge successfully. We had made the right choice.

I later learned that problems with fishhooks and line are not uncommon among eagles. We hear much about the damage they do to pelicans, loons, and other water-birds, but here was a case where a lost line could have killed a bird some distance from any open water, and every year eaglets with such problems are found in nests.

When visiting that same nest I learned that there can be a large size difference between eagle young. Firstborn birds are always further along in development, and if the firstborn happens to be a larger female and the secondborn a male, the size difference is compounded. If there were to be any conflict between the birds, it would be in this situation, but both eaglets were well fed and completely unaggressive toward each other.

✳ ✳ ✳

The older eaglet on the right was fed fish that was tethered by monofilament line, a common problem for eagles. The line is visible coming from the left corner of the bird's mouth and wrapping around the left wing. While at this nest I got a close-up view of the size difference between the eaglets, which is especially pronounced when the firstborn is a female and secondborn is a male.

Ramage-stage eaglets at five weeks of age. Now feathered for protection, the eaglets are able to move well around the nest and have just started to tear up their own food and feed themselves.

Young eagles at seven weeks of age. They lead a fairly solitary nest life at this stage, when the parents may visit only once a day to leave food for them.

My eaglets had changed dramatically in the two weeks I took to get back to them. A uniform layer of brown feathering almost completely covered their bodies, and the birds were much more alert and close to being able to stand up. Definitions vary as to when an "eaglet" becomes an "eagle." But these five-week-old birds exhibited a dramatic change from the nestlings I had previously observed. Clearly they were on their way to becoming eagles.

This midpoint in their nest-bound life was the start of the weaning-away process from their parents. In comparison to the down that covers eaglets, the body feathering of juveniles provides far better insulation against cool weather and good protection from the sun, rain, and other elements. Up until now one of the parents had always been at the nest to provide this protection, but gradually the adults spent more and more time perched in nearby roost trees, always ready to fly to the nest should danger threaten, but far enough away to not call attention to their young.

The nest cup that held the eggs and downy young had slowly been filling in, and now the nest surface was fairly flat. This gave the young eagles less confinement, and they shuffled about the nest, strengthening their leg muscles until they were able to stand. (Usually eaglets are able to stand at five or six weeks of age, a stage of development falconers refer to as the "ramage" stage.) Once the young eagles are able to stand, they can tear their food and feed themselves. The parents still bring food to the nest daily, but the young eagles' behavior changes. When in the eyas stage of development, the eaglets' begging calls were followed by the parent tearing off small pieces of food and gingerly offering it to the youngsters. In the ramage stage, the young eagles become more and more aggressive. By seven weeks of age, the adult may quickly depart as soon as it has brought food because the young eagles aggressively snatch the prey from their parent.

This is the stage at which nests can become untidy. The young eagles are not as thorough in completely eating what is brought, and bits and pieces of unconsumed prey fall down into the cracks and crevices of the nest, creating a build-up of food in the nest, all of which attracts flies and gives some nests an unpleasant air.

The juvenile eagles are eight weeks of age and exercising their wings in preparation for flight.

By seven weeks of age, young eagles have attained almost their full fledging weight and very much look ready to fly. But through my lens I could see that the tail feathers had only begun to lengthen and wing feathers were far from fledging length. Indeed, much of the growth that occurred in the next three weeks was channeled into wing and tail feathers, because these largest of eagle feathers would have to support the birds on their first flight.

* * *

In late June the eagles were eight weeks old. At this stage they were up on their feet most of the time and had begun exercising their growing wings, strengthening the pectoral muscles that would power them. It is at this stage that eagles commonly fall out of nests. (I observed one eagle back up to the edge of a nest to defecate, as always facing into the wind to avoid the excrement blowing back onto it, when a sudden gust of wind came up. Reflexively the eagle spread its wings for balance and was lifted up a few feet and almost blown off the nest.) Wing flapping seems to be stimulated by the wind, and many eagles probably spend their last week or two on the ground or on a branch below the nest. They are able to glide to the ground, usually without damage, and their hunger calls allow the adults to locate them when bringing food. Unless the eagles are injured or unduly exposed to people or predators, they will be fine out of the nest, and the general thinking is to leave them alone.

This eight-week stage is about the latest time eagles are handled by banders. Prior to this, the young eagles will hold their ground in response to any disturbance in the nest. But from eight weeks of age on, they are much more likely to jump from the nest if any sort of disturbance or danger comes their way.

Nine-week-old brancher-stage juveniles. The feathers are still developing at this stage. The tip of a feather develops first, and the base is the last to develop. Until the feather is completely grown, the shaft or quill, which is filled with blood during growth, is soft, quite delicate, and is not firmly attached to the underlying wing bones. Falconers refer to raptors during feather growth as being "in the blood." Once the shafts are blood-free and attached to the bone (known as "hard-penned" to falconers), they can withstand a lot more pressure and the bird is ready for vigorous flight.

Look closely at this bird's beak, and you will see a piece of white down stuck there. Although much of the natal down is pushed out by the feathers that are coming in, some down remains attached to the bird's body, and during the last two or three weeks of nest life the young eagle spends a fair amount of time preening out this down with its bill.

During the brancher stage, the juveniles fly to nearby roosts. It is thought that they use this period to strengthen their grip. A strong grip will become crucial when they will have to clasp their own food, such as fish. At this nine week age, the wings have yet to fully grow. When the wings are finally grown, they will extend to within one inch of the tip of the tail.

For their first flight's destination, juvenile eagles generally choose a nearby roost tree, such as this pine, from which the adults have plucked sprigs to line the nest. Such plucking also creates an unobstructed perch to view the surroundings. A week after leaving nest, the young eagles remain near the nest, entirely dependent on their parents for food. Hunger calls enable the parents to locate the young.

My eagles met no such misfortune. By the Fourth of July weekend they had taken to the support branches of their nest to further strengthen their legs and improve their balance and coordination. Thus they passed from the ramage stage to the "brancher" stage of development. Their tails had almost completely grown, but the longest primary flight feathers still had a good five inches to grow. In another week they would take their first flight, although the wings would not be completely grown for this first venture. I marked the ten-week point on my calendar, the typical point of fledging, and made sure I was in my blind for this special day.

An eagle eyrie is a quiet, tranquil place—except on the day of fledging. Although many eagles leave the nest accidentally by being blown over or falling, those that remain are very much attached to their homes, and some coaxing may be necessary to get them to leave. As with all birds of prey, food is the control and the reward the parents use for this. For several days prior to fledging, the parents did not bring food to the nest, but rather perched nearby with the enticement. The begging calls of the young became screams as they darted from one edge of the nest to the other and out onto their home tree's branches. The moment of fledging came unexpectedly: A sudden gust of wind knocked the first young eagle into the air. As is natural for eagle fledglings, it glided to one of the roost trees it had seen its parents on in the past few months, where a meal, it hoped, awaited.

The young eagles stayed close to the nest during the next few weeks. I'm sure this was in part to let their wings develop fully. Even after the young eagle's wings are completely grown, it will take an additional week for the blood to leave the shafts of the feathers and the feathers to become firmly attached to the underlying bone. Until this happens, vigorous flight could be damaging to the feathers. Up to five weeks are required from the time young eagles leave the nest until their flight feathers are completely formed. This period is used not only to complete feather growth, but also to develop muscle strength and improve flying skills.

✳ ✳ ✳

First flight.

The ten weeks of nest life can be divided into three stages: *eyas, which is derived from the French* niais, *meaning "fresh from the nest," and which refers to the first three to five weeks when the eaglet is covered with down, needs to be brooded frequently, and is unable to stand and feed itself;* ramage, *from the French word of the same spelling meaning "wild" or "of the branches," when the eaglet becomes covered by feathers, needs to be brooded only in harsh weather, and learns to stand up, hold food, and feed itself; and* brancher, *which for eagles is the one-week period near the nine- to ten-week age when they move out to the branches to strengthen their leg muscles and fine-tune their balance.*

In both scientific and popular usage, the terms eaglet *and* eagle *denote different ages. Technically, a young bird from birth all the way to the point that it is independent of its parents (up to ten weeks after it leaves the nest) is an eaglet. In practice, however, the term* eaglet *is usually used for only the eyas and ramage stages. The youngster is called an* eagle *when it reaches the brancher stage of nest life. In practice, brancher-stage eagles are also called* juveniles, *although technically* juvenile *refers to the first coat of feathering that grows in, which is brown—almost red in certain light. At the end of its first year, when it molts much of its juvenile plumage, the eagle is known as an immature eagle, although the word* immature *also encompasses the first-year juvenile plumage. You may also hear the term* subadult, *which could be used to mean any eagle younger than adult age, but is customarily used to mean plumages that occur between the juvenile and adult plumages.*

It doesn't seem possible that this bird will soon migrate. All migration carries some risk, and adult eagles tend to stay on their home range as long as food and water are available. Immature eagles do a lot of shuffling around; it's one of the reasons for their higher mortality rate when compared to adults. An eagle that hatches in the winter in Florida might well spend its first summer in Canada, for instance, before returning to Florida in the fall. Eagles that nest in the Great Lakes states and south central Canada often spend their winters along the open waters of the Mississippi and its tributaries. Birds from interior Canada may go to the coasts, and large numbers congregate in Glacier National Park. Eagles are by nature lazy birds, and an easier-to-get food supply is an incentive for them to move around.

The unfolding of my young eagles into adults went as planned. The parents continued to bring food daily, either directly to the young, being guided by their hunger calls, or to the nest to which the young would quickly come from a nearby tree. The young were still totally dependent on their parents for food. But every day their wings were stronger; their soaring flight took them higher and higher. By the end of August, they were well out of the nest territory. I'd occasionally see them flying over my house, but short of my sprouting wings there was no way I could keep good track of them.

They will likely leave their parents' home range in September, traveling irregularly and unpredictably. Their first fifteen weeks of life, with the constant protection and care of their parents, were a paradise to what will confront them with the approach of the first winter. They will be on their own when it comes to locating and catching prey. Colder weather increases eagles' food requirements, and shorter days give them less time to obtain sufficient food. In addition to learning hunting techniques, the immature bald eagles will have to learn what type of prey to hunt— and what not to hunt. First-year eagles are notorious for attacking just about anything that floats or moves. I've seen them go after my duck decoys and have seen them stoop on trumpeter swans, birds more than capable of defending themselves. In most cases, such mistakes do no harm and are lessons learned. Attack an animal like a porcupine, however, and the mistake could be fatal.

✳ ✳ ✳

Lessons and dangers such as these have been with the bald eagle for millions of years. They are part of the natural system of checks and balances that regulates all life. But in the past three hundred years, humankind has added additional roadblocks with which my two young eagles will have to contend. As with many other species, loss of suitable habitat is by far the biggest problem they'll have to deal with. For bald eagles, suitable habitat means large trees in areas free of disturbance, especially during the early part of nesting, for support of nests, protection from predators, and room for roosting. It means an adequate supply of food, mainly fish, which in turn means access to water.

In the Northwoods, logging during the 1800s severely reduced the number of suitable nest trees because the large pines the eagles favored were also the chopper's prime targets. Settlement followed logging, and the increase in human activity interfered with those birds that did attempt to nest. Use of organochlorine pesticides like DDE and DDT after World War II contaminated water supplies, the poisons concentrating in the fat of organisms along the food chain until, by the time they reached the bald eagle at the top of the food chain, amounts were high enough to prevent successful reproduction. These pesticides interfered with the birds' calcium metabolism to the point that eggshells thinned and lacked enough strength to prevent crushing during incubation. In high enough concentrations, DDT and dieldrin, another insecticide, can directly kill bald eagles; in the 1960s, almost 10 percent of known bald eagle deaths were attributed to dieldrin poisoning.

The situation is now a bit better for my young eagles. Controlled logging practices and regrowth of the clear-cut forest the loggers left a century ago has greatly increased the number of suitable nest trees. Both the government and private landowners have established buffer zones around existing nest trees, areas where disturbance is minimized or not allowed (my blind was one-eighth mile from the eyrie, just outside one of the critical buffer zones). And because of banning, pesticides have slowly been flushed from our environment during the past twenty years.

A group of immature eagles feeding on a large pike that floated up onto the ice during spring breakup in front of my house. Note the difference in plumages during the first four years of life. Eagles do not have a complete, well-defined molt each year. Rather, feathers are lost throughout the year, although mainly in the summer, and not all feathers are lost in a given year. Individual feathers or little clumps of them may persist for two or even three years, and the bleaching action of the sun fades these feathers to the point of producing unusual coloring patterns. Eagles must be able to fly the year-round. Therefore, unlike ducks and some other birds who lose all their flight feathers at once and regain their new ones in a few weeks, eagles do not molt more than two or three flight feathers at a time. Adult eagles typically start their flight-feather molt during incubation and may not complete it until the fall.

Other man-made problems persist. In spite of international protection by the Migratory Bird Treaty Act, federal protection for the bald eagle itself as well as for endangered and threatened species, and state protection, the bald eagle is persecuted by shooting, which remains the greatest known cause of death for bald eagles. Another danger: Bait left in an uncovered trap is irresistible to a bald eagle, and in spite of more widespread use of covered traps, dozens of eagles are recovered every year with crippling trap injuries. Increasing amounts of PCBs and mercury in our lakes,

A golden eagle.

in part brought about by acid rain, can be fatal to bald eagle embryos and young. In the 1980s, lead shot was shown to be fatal to bald eagles who had consumed it along with the injured or dead waterfowl the shot was originally intended for. Even if insufficient to kill the eagle, lead would often weaken the bird and expose it to more generalized diseases and predation. Nontoxic steel shot is now in use throughout most of North America, but the tons of lead remaining at the bottoms of our waterways will persist for many years to come.

The bald eagle has also shown some adaptability to human activity; as the lakeshores they commonly frequented have been developed, many eagle pairs have moved inland along adjoining rivers and have successfully nested in these more isolated areas.

If either of my young eagles survives these hurdles, it will likely congregate with other eagles along the open waters of the Mississippi and other rivers during the winter. In the spring, my eagles and some of their neighbors will return to this forested nest area in northern Wisconsin. The response of their parents will vary from a hesitant acceptance—in a few cases they may even be fed by the adults—to aggressive rejection out of the territory. This homing instinct is, however, an advantage in situations where a population needs to be increased. Eaglets from Alaska, Minnesota, and Wisconsin have been moved to many less-populated states. The eagles have adopted these new sites as their home because that is where they learned to fly.

Most of my young eagles' feathers will be molted at the end of their first year, the richly colored new feathers contrasting with the faded and worn old feathers that remain. And again, at the end of the second year, another less-than-complete molt will result. The appearances of these "salt and pepper" plumages are highly variable, depending in large part on how complete each molt is as well as how much sunlight and subsequent fading the older feathers are exposed to. But slowly, my eagles' appearance will become more and more distinctive, and at the end of the third year an ospreylike plumage appears. Most of the eagle's head will turn white, but a dark band of feathers will persist through the eye. The tail will be more white than it was previously, the dark brown eye will become more hazel, and the base of the beak more yellow. Adulthood will be near.

In the fourth year, the iris of the eye will change to yellow in a matter of a few weeks. Some dark feathering may persist in the tail and head, but it will be noticeable only from close up, and a trace of black will remain at the tip of the bill. Most birds will have paired by now and will attempt nesting. Sexual maturity does not always arrive at the same time as the adult plumage does, and successful nesting (defined here as eggs being laid) may not occur until the bird is five or six years of age. I remember observing a four-year-old female at another eyrie who was adult in many ways except for the black at the tip of her beak. Nest refurbishing occurred normally, but she failed to adopt the soliciting posture necessary for reproduction. The male could only hop to one side of her and then the other, and mating did not occur.

Many difficulties will face my young eagles. If the statistics hold true, only one of them will survive to the next summer, and that one will have only a 20 percent chance of making it to adulthood and nesting. But if one survives to that age, the world will be at its feet. An adult eagle has successfully dealt with just about everything humans and nature can throw at it. When I see a white head and yellow eye, I'm looking at one smart, tough bird, a bird that will nest for ten, twenty years or more, enough to replace itself in the big scheme of things.

❋ ❋ ❋

I last saw my eagles in late August, soaring a few hundred feet up in the air on one of the summer's last thermals. A million challenges and experiences lie before them, but if they can successfully beat the odds, what a life they will have in comparison to my earthbound existence. It's an unusual feeling to see a mighty eagle high up in the air and know it's the same helpless ugly duckling I held in my hands only three months before (and saw created shortly before that). That day I knew what parents must feel like when two of their kids leave the house and gain their independence.

There is no confusing an adult bald eagle with any other species. An occasional golden eagle of similar size wanders through the Great Lakes states in the winter, but the golden eagle's much darker head and tail allow for a clear distinction between the bald eagle and its distant cousin. Golden eagles are commonly confused with immature bald eagles, however. One sure way to distinguish between the two is to look at the eagles' feet. The feathering of a golden eagle's feet extends all the way down to its toes, while a bald eagle's feathering stops halfway between the ankle and the base of the toes. In other words, the foot of a bald eagle has comparatively more scales than feathers. Another interesting difference: Golden eagles have longer tails and wider wings than bald eagles of similar size have. Wider wings and a longer tail give the golden eagle more maneuverability in comparison to a bald eagle, something of a benefit to a golden eagle because almost all of its hunting is for quick-footed, agile mammals such as rabbits. This shows an immature eagle in the four-year-old "osprey" plumage. The eagle's bill is yellow except for the black tip; its eye, hazel in this picture, is starting to turn from deep brown to yellow.

The old nest tree, knocked down by an autumn wind.
An eagle flight feather points skyward for the seedling pine.

The broken-off trunk of the nest tree.

Epilogue

My last trip to the blind came in early September. With the eagles now on their own and some distance from the nest, it was safe for me to make the walk in daylight. A few mopping-up duties were in order, but one more climb up the old pine to retrieve the blind and lens and I'd have some time left over to reminisce.

Many things went through my mind that day. I thought of the first time I saw the parent eagles on my lake some ten years ago. Beyond the wealth of experience that no amount of writing and photography can adequately communicate, I thought of all the things they'd shown me about life and living. I thought about the limitless number of other similar dramas that are played out in the natural world every day without our realization. I had already edited down some fifteen hundred hours of photography to a select a hundred images that covered the eagles' nest history, but at an average of one-thirtieth of a second per exposure, the one hundred represented a total of little more than three seconds of time. I thought about that a lot: A tiny fraction of their lifetime in my hands, a drop of water in the ocean, a few stars in a universe of billions, yet how much richer I was for it.

I took a walk over to give the nest tree a final pat, and was surprised to find that its trunk had snapped off about fifteen feet above the ground, probably the result of an August windstorm. That tree had seemed so impregnable to me; a dozen generations of humanity had come and gone since its birth, and countless numbers of eagles probably have used it as their home, starting at the time of Jefferson.

As I looked around the haggard tree's base, I saw that a seedling pine had sprouted. Alongside lay an adult eagle flight feather, shielding the youngster and pointing its way skyward. It's only fitting, I thought, considering the many generations of eagles the parent pine had protected. Every part of nature depends on and interacts with all the other parts in ways we can only imagine.

Perhaps in another century this young pine will, in its turn, play host to future eagles. But that September, both the parent tree's lifetime and my season with the eagles had come to an end.

The author. Photo © by Mary Ann Grymala.

Notes on the Photography

To take these one-of-a-kind photographs, Scott Nielsen used a 2500 Meade Schmidt-Cassegrain f/10 lens, adding to that a Nikon TC-200 teleconverter for many of the photos. All exposure were taken with Nikon F3 camera bodies and MD-4 motor drives. His film of choice was Kodachrome 64, and exposures ranged from $\frac{1}{125}$ second on bright, sunlit days to $\frac{1}{8}$ second on overcast days. During the cold days of March and April, a remote battery pack was used, allowing Nielsen to keep the batteries warm. Without such an accessory, prolonged exposure to the Wisconsin cold would have reduced the batteries' power to the point that cameras would not have worked.

Resources

Each season brings updates in our knowledge of the bald eagle and changes for bald eagle managers. Among the many worthy information sources are The Raptor Research Foundation, The Raptor Center, and The National Wildlife Federation.

The Raptor Research Foundation
James Fitzpatrick
Carpenter Nature Center
12805 St. Croix Trail
Hastings, MN 55033

The Raptor Center
1920 Firch Avenue
St. Paul, MN 55108
(612) 624-4745

Institute for Wildlife Research
National Wildlife Federation
1400 Sixteenth Street Northwest
Washington, D.C. 20036
(For inquiries by telephone, call their Virginia number: (703) 790-4484.)

Index

The author preparing to climb an eagle nest tree to band the young. He is strapping on the climbing irons necessary to reach the first branches. Note the eagle feathers littering the area. Adults start their molt in April, and by the time the tree was visited in late May, dozens of feathers were on the ground. The tree behind the author is about the size of tree eagles select for their nests, typically two to four feet in diameter at its base and eighty to 140 feet tall.

About the Author

Dr. Scott Nielsen is an avian taxidermist and photographer specializing in waterfowl and birds of prey. He holds degrees and advanced training from the University of Wisconsin, University of Arizona, and Northwestern University. While at Northwestern, he studied under Leon Pray at the Field Museum of Natural History and was able to prepare many of the world's rarest birds, including remounting specimens of the now extinct Labrador duck and passenger pigeon.

Since 1968 his studio has been located near the historic portage between the St. Croix and Brule rivers in northwestern Wisconsin. Although much of his photography is done in far-reaching places, most is taken within a few miles of his isolated home. Two pairs of bald eagles and dozens of songbird species nest within walking distance, and a wood duck nest box project begun in 1974 now has an average of forty hens successfully nesting in a five-square-mile area centered at the studio.

Dr. Nielsen's photography has appeared in virtually every North American outdoor and nature publication, plus numerous calendars, posters, books, and sportswear products. Seventeen different limited edition lithographs have been produced, of which eleven are sold out. His work "Exploding Into Spring" has sold over 46,000 prints in an open-ended edition, with the original being purchased for a five-figure sum that rivals the highest price ever paid for a photograph.

Since 1988 Nielsen has been the contract photographer for Ducks Unlimited, an international organization dedicated to preserving and restoring the world's wetlands and its associated wildlife.